The Only Thing I Like About Living

(Three Steps to Freedom from Solitude, Boredom, and Addiction in Adulthood)

Written By:
Jay M. Horne
2018
Bradenton, FL

The Only Thing I Like About Living

Jay Horne

The Only Thing I Like About Living. Copyright © 2018 by Jay Mathis Horne. All rights reserved, including the right to reproduce this work in any form whatsoever, without permission in writing from the author, except for brief passages in connection with a review.

Cataloguing Publication Data
Horne, Jay M., 1980-
The Only Thing I Like About Living / Jay M. Horne
ISBN: 978-0-9963227-0-6
Library of Congress Control Number: 2018908963

Bookflurry Publishing does not participate in, endorse, or have any authority or responsibility concerning private business affairs between the author and the public.
All mail addressed to the author will be forwarded but the publisher cannot, unless specifically instructed by the author, give out an address or phone number.

Bookflurry.com
Bradenton, FL

The Only Thing I Like About Living

FOREWORD

As Jim Gaffigan said on his comedy tour, and it applies to everything in adult life,

"It's funny how our out look on alcohol changes during our lifetime. It starts out as something we know is wrong. As teenagers we say, 'I don't really like the taste of it, but it's kinda cool,' then it turns into something we think gives us confidence to fit in with the opposite sex during our early twenties, and by the time we reach our forties we're like, "Ya know what, this is the only thing I like about being alive."

He roused a laugh at that statement, but only because it's true.

There are so many of us who smile nowadays without getting our eyes involved because we come home from work to our kids or significant other, and that's what we think, "This is the only thing I like about being alive." Whether it is a drink, a person, a substance, a bowl of ice cream, a daily jog, masturbation, or even just the trip from work to home, as humans we struggle not to end up in a place of existence when we're holding onto just one thing for meaning or to get us through another day. Breaking the boredom of repetitive experience and maintaining a colorful imagination is what it all boils down to.

I am the worst kind of addict because my addiction has to do with my spirituality. Drinking and drugs opened my mind to the divine; sometimes through the half-life of the substance, and other times through the thankfulness that I lived through another use or bender.

After all of my previous books on defeating addiction through spirituality were published, I thought that I would be through it. Perhaps I felt as if, I had shown the world that my addictions had done some good for others, that I could now rest and be cured? Yet, a wise man once said, "It is a dangerous fallacy to believe that we can rest upon our achievements."

After all of my accomplishments, The boredom got to me and I couldn't help but eventually landing myself in AA, again.

Through writing this book, I've been able to identify my addictive personality, based on past experience, as an insatiable desire for imbalance. Many years ago I read that the spirit desires movement in any form and deplores stagnation. The idea stems from the evidence that there can be no growth without movement in one direction or another and the recognition that perfectly balanced forces result in a net movement of zero. This idea of Constructive Imbalance, I finally came to realize, is something that I attribute to my near impossible ability to relax.

    Being sober and in the company of other drunks has given me a real sense of why myself and others struggle with that, not just in our workplace, but all day, and in everything. Why do we think alcohol, tobacco, and prescription drug abuse are the world's favorite pass times? They are our feeble attempts at enhancing an experience that has become otherwise boring. Ask anyone sitting around the circle at an AA meeting and you will see that after a length of time experiencing the effects of these substances we come to realize, often scraping the bottom, that they too are simply experiences which eventually can become old and colorless.

    The amazing thing about boredom is that it is an illusion. It manifests itself in a way that is easily misinterpreted by the mind in today's fast paced world. Boredom really is just a way the spirit gently reminds us that it desires new information. The illusion that things become stale and motionless is easily broken through the right thinking. As Marcel Proust said, and little do we realize, "The great voyage of discovery comes not in seeking new landscapes but in having new eyes."

Jay Horne

TABLE OF CONTENTS

Foreword	PAGE 5
Introduction	PAGE 11
Why It Works for Everyone	PAGE 13
Solitude	PAGE 17
Boredom	PAGE 27
Peace & Serenity	PAGE 33
Happiness	PAGE 39
Intention	PAGE 49
Addiction	PAGE 53
Overcome	PAGE 57
The Promises	PAGE 61
The Steps	PAGE 67
A Note on Suicide	PAGE 73
Resources	PAGE 79
My Personal Beliefs and a Note on Enlightenment	PAGE 81
Thank You	PAGE 89
Referenced Hyperlinks	PAGE 91

The Only Thing I Like About Living

Jay Horne

for
all those sick and suffering and their families.

A special thanks to the Serenity Room and all of its members who are brave and strong enough to share everyday. You truly make a difference.

The Only Thing I Like About Living

INTRODUCTION

Just imagine that you could take all of the stuff in the universe and put it into a great big mortar and pestle to grind up into tiny pieces and then send it through a sift. Now put all of that back into a grinder and repeat the process of reducing it even further. Sift it again and then try and pick out the single atom which holds the key to happiness, the color black or white. There is no single iota that is amazing in and of itself. Only belief can make the matter of the universe ever able to be something that it isn't. Still, our souls can grow during strong emotions like love or excitement in ways that make the most amazing and colorful substances in the universe seem dull by comparison when they cease to be looked upon with awe. The mind is what does the labeling through perception, and the experience is what tells us if it is awesome.

It's almost as if the body is playing a balancing act between the mind and the soul. The soul is like a scale which likes to be Helter-skelter. Meanwhile the body and mind try and keep it in perfect balance by adding weight to the trays. Why does this conflict exist? Perfect balance is stagnation, without imbalance there can be no real movement, and without movement there can be no growth. I think our soul always yearns for growth.

I can almost pinpoint when I started falling victim to this trap of stagnant thinking. My dad moved us around a lot as kids, which meant we had the extreme pleasure of making new friends in every great public school we attended. I am pretty sure by junior high that I had grown less than excited about telling someone about myself. The first time you are easily duped into being excited for a fresh start with new people, but after having the same conversation for the third time, trying to sum up the entirety of your lifelong personality to match yourself as someone's new best instafriend, you lose all interest in trying.

If you've already survived your twenties then you know what I mean. We've all felt this way while dating. Eventually you just start making shit up on a first date, because there's only so many times you can genuinely put true emotion behind saying the same exact thing during the same exact experience. There's nothing worst than the feeling that your coming off as fake just because you've done something a thousand times. It reaches a point where you start thinking that the original thing you did is now the bad thing, and the bad thing you didn't do might just be better- at least it will be genuine... how's that for an oxymoron?

The old adage about not being able to step into the same river twice may be true, but how do we keep this in mind when we step through at the same spot fifty times?

This is where it is important to sometimes take a good look at how we generalize people as we get older. Together we are going to identify the thinking that has driven our solitary, boring, and addictive personalities. We are going to determine why our favorite vices, though we know they are bad, make us feel so young and good again. We'll exercise three steps that will permanently purge us of these choke holds. Then, by introducing three simple ingredients into our lives, we will discover why it is so hard to leave our childhood behind and why doing just that is the most rewarding thing we may ever experience.

The three ingredients I am going to remind you of are every human being's birthright. Halfway through writing this book I looked back and decided to make a outline for it to be sure I remembered to cover as much information as possible. I've always been a working class individual and the last thing I want is to put out a product that, has the potential to help millions of everyday working Joes like me, but just wastes their time and money. After looking at the outline, I was reluctant to restructure the manuscript into a book that reads like a program, because, while that is what it may turn out to be, I want it also to be entertaining, inspiring, and most of all, original and true.

It is with that, that I would like to promise you that I have included all the information that is important to this subject, but have left the whole in a story-like form so that a guy like me can pick it up, start reading, and stay interested instead of flipping back and forth looking for quick answers. The answer must come along the journey, for knowledge unearned, most often, goes unremembered.

Jay Horne

WHY IT WORKS FOR EVERYONE

What gets people into an AA meeting? Every story is unique, and mine is no better than another's. The genuine nature of each person's story is part of what makes AA so effective, so I'm not in a hurry to share my own here. That is an experience best left to your own meeting. Every individual experiences and extracts a different meaning from the stories they hear while attending an AA meeting. That is why every third person who speaks of how they overcame their addiction urges newcomers to just keep coming back. The meaning and worth of the meetings is something that grows like a vine. When the first flower blooms on the vine of your experience there, an understanding will start taking hold. Perhaps you finally comprehend the meaning of serenity, or during your third meeting you happen to hear someone's story that solidifies a deep belief that you've been building years over... One thing is for certain, when it starts to happen, you will know it.

I attend a lot of open discussion meetings, and from experience, I can say that ninety percent of the time someone chooses the topic of spirituality. If someone doesn't directly bring it up, the subject is danced around until the gravity from the spinning idea sucks everyone right in. This is the reason why I say I am the worst. My addictions are like keys to my spiritual link, as crazy as that sounds; and though they are my demons and inevitable downfall—I love them. Dangerous, I know.

So how can I ever be free of addiction if the key to being free has so much to do with spirituality? AA has a convenient way to brush off this question by stating that you must give up your control to a power greater than yourself *however you understand it*. But this doesn't ever help recovering addicts identify a power, or understand it. As a matter of fact, I dare to say that understanding your higher power, while possible, is an extreme exercise of study and takes a certain kind of individual to even have an interest in such an endeavor. All in all, understanding your higher power, is not necessary. However, having one, for not so obvious reasons, is. So what about the Atheists? What about people like me, who are not Atheists, but rather are Gnostics (one's who know beyond all doubt what the highest power is)? Are they to be neglected; sent away to some other program or doctor to figure out? The answer is no.

Mainstream religious followers, even Agnostics (someone who knows that there is something out there, but not sure what it is) we seem to think would have an easier time praying to a 'God' during their recovery. But that is not always the case. Individuals who follow a denomination may not necessarily believe that their idea of God makes the world go around, or that their God is intrinsically only good.

Sometimes even those who follow a creed don't have a conscience.

The people among these denominations who find recovery the easiest are always the ones who are an *active* part of a religious community. In that knowledge, it becomes apparent that their belief in a God to pray too, isn't what helps them, it is that they have peers with whom to relate and unfold their story of internal belief.

It is the same with an AA meeting. Simply being around other people, even alcoholics or addicts, who open up and talk, makes way for an avenue of discovery. The discovery to where this avenue leads comes from one's own past experiences but the bridges and pathways cannot be constructed without a network of malleable sources of information for the universe to do its work. The best wild cards of information happen to be people, because you never can tell what might come out of their mouths.

Why are non-denominational churches the fastest growing community congregations in the world? Look at their platform. They have become the most vaguely directed sermon delivery systems ever concocted. Most of their content is based around helping the community, accepting others where they are, and positive thinking. Open arms to sinners and saints a like. An accepting that Jesus frees us from our sins by his sacrifice in the past is all it takes to fast track your way into the inner circle. The promise of love, no matter what you've done, a wide support system of friends in the community, and a place to gather and meet others.

Opening a church is like opening a McDonald's. It's become a franchise. You buy a business model, funnel some of the earning s to the top dogs, and have an endless supply of media, projects, programs, kid's camps, and support to spread

'The Word'. None of this is bad. As stated before, there is no need to understand our higher power, the key is in finding one that works for us. And for some, most, it seems, it's right there.

No one has ever accomplished anything on their own. The truth in that one statement alone should portray to us that two people are in-fact more powerful than one. They say to never underestimate the power of stupid people in large groups. A power greater than the self can be found in any congregation. That's why AA works.

The path of knowledge is a forced one. In order to learn we must be pushed. On the path of knowledge we are always fighting something, avoiding something, preparing for something, and that something is always inexplicable- greater and more powerful than us.
—Carlos Castaneda

That something; the path to knowledge, is what some believe is the very thing that is more powerful than themselves. Not a separate entity who presides over but rather the totality of the group of people they are a part of. The key is that it only shows itself through relationships (no matter how minor) with other human beings. Simply sitting among others and listening can manifest an understanding of the self. A room full of people from different beliefs, who have overcome a variety of addictions, is a powerful tool for any person that doesn't feel joy in everyday living. If joy is missing from most things in your life, there is no other reason than that it is being placed too heavily into another single part of your existence.

The only thing I like about living is having a drink and relaxing.

The only thing I like about living is driving to and from work.

The only thing I like about living is seeing that girl who works at the gas station.

The only thing I like about living is spending time with my kids.

The only thing I like about living is going to bed at night.

The only thing I *dislike* about living is being sober.

The Only Thing I Like About Living

Jay Horne

SOLITUDE

The Only Thing I Like About Living

1

The more we strive for conviviality, companionship, and release from boredom through an addiction, the lonelier we eventually become, but why?

An alcoholic of over 32 years sober, once admitted that she had had a few beers two days in a row after she moved down to the area from up north. She stopped it at that, and returned to an AA meeting, but couldn't help but ask herself why she would sacrifice all of her time sober for such a little escapade.

Many people think, after a given amount of time they are no longer an addict or alcoholic, just to find out the opposite all over again. The truth is, people who are not addicts or alcoholics just aren't there yet. They will be, it is only a matter of time.

The act of drinking or drugging to enhance a colorful imagination, stave off worry, or increase social interaction is, in many ways like a spiritual undertaking. There are three kinds of people in it. Those who don't know (the kids), those who think they know (the teen drinkers), and those who know (the alcoholics, or *adults*). 'Those who don't know' need no alcohol or drug to have a good time enjoying life, they just live and enjoy it. 'Those who think they know' drink and drug with no real understanding to where it will lead. 'Those who know', have been where it leads and drinking with those who think they know will lead to nothing more than irritability of misunderstanding from those drinkers, and eventually to leading by example (falling off the wagon).

It is scary to 'those who think they know' when they are getting close to real knowing, because they can't see their lives without alcohol. They can't see their selves hanging out with "sober" people, and being boring the rest of their lives. But the drinker who still is counted among the ones 'who think they know', doesn't yet realize that the "sober people" are not boring folks at all; the people they envision do not exist. What they are picturing is a manifestation of their fear and generalizing about the public who happen to be their only key to sober communion.

The alcoholic, or 'the ones who know', never want a drink... they want enough drink to be drunk. The people that blooming Recoverees imagine as the "sober, boring people" is in fact, everyone. It is the kids who don't drink and who know not of drinking. It is the teens, young adults, and adults who drink to enhance their experiences and stave their worries. And yes, it is further still, the non-drinkers, the addicts who choose not to get drunk because they fit not into the younger (in alcohol years) classifications.

    The 32 year sober alcoholic who decided to pick up a drink with her new acquaintances did so without realizing that these three classifications of drinkers existed. But by the end of her second outing with her new friends she marginally suspected that she was drinking with people who may not have yet shared her experience with alcohol. Luckily she realized it early enough not to go on and get drunk. She saw herself, in her mind, reliving all those years again when she was competing to be the most sober person among friends while drinking the most. Then remembered she had already won that contest, and reaped its ill rewards as the experience of alcoholism. She returned to an AA meeting to get some numbers of the fellow senior drunks, because they are the ones who know where it leads.

    Despite how it sounds, it was not that she was making friends with the wrong people. If she had a full understanding of the classifications of drinkers and addicts, she would have realized that she was trying to be the wrong person among younger alcoholics. She needn't drink a drink with them, because that was relating on a false level of her experience. You can't be drinking a drink and represent where it will lead them. You can't be the best at drinking twice.

    It's not as if you are a spy and need to disguise yourself as a friendly in enemy territory to get your information. You're drinking to get drunk. If not, you're just a spy. If you've lived through the drinking and drugging days, there is no getting them back. Represent that. Do it by not drinking and being yourself, because that is truly what will one day be best for them to. Don't fool them, because they will end up thinking the addiction is telling the truth later in life as well. When it comes down to it, you really have to be true to yourself and others when it comes to addictions, and the only way to do that is to be respectful of people at their own stage of addiction and alcoholism. Respecting their stage means not pretending to still be part of it.

Jay Horne

Respecting other people's development, and being true to yourself can apply to everything in life. There are sports fans who have experienced their team win the Superbowl that experienced a sustained uplifted existence for days as if they were in heaven. Artists in the 60's tripped on LSD and other psychedelics, every time reaching another plateau, would go weeks on unstimulated highs because they had figured out some new secret to the universe. Heroin addicts today die by the dozens in cities across the country because they are chasing that same experience again and again.

When you fail to understand that the mind and body grow with unique experiences, you risk falling into the trap of repetition. The feelings of elation that come with unique experiences, especially those associated with accomplishment are dangerous caveats the brain uses as rewards. Like the ching a slot machine makes on bingo. But the growth of ones perception eventually returns to an even keel and the person who experienced the jackpot sometimes tries figuring out how they did it. The elation they seek is the holy grail, and some die in search of it. The truth that lies beneath the experience is that it was simply a stage in life. Dumb it down a little, and it was just a stage or step in drinking. We're only young once folks.

At home we can we the best drunk all by ourselves, but we can't be the best drinker out there in public anymore. At risk of sounding like an admonition, we already were the best at that, our time has passed. Be happy with 'having been' and be the best You now. There's nothing worse than being negatively labeled a 'Has been', yet there's nothing more enlightening than sitting in a room full of those who know that is exactly who they are.

It's okay to be a Has been. There's more to be out there, and we should be proud of what we've lived through. We become Hermits when we can't let go and instead wait around like a caterpillar in a cocoon for some metamorphosis back into what we used to be. For people, metamorphosis takes place through relationships not alienation, and time only goes forward.

The Only Thing I Like About Living

2

Nowadays the majority of our relationships boil down to clicks and likes. Our best friends from childhood are pictures in our feeds and touch-and-go comments or infrequent instant messages. Our lives draw in as we trim activities to make room for those closest to us. Our spouse, our kids, and our employment all need special attention as we navigate through the uncharted waters of growing an adult life. During this time in our experience on earth, many of us have to make difficult choices when it comes to the things that we borrow that time from. Often our passions, which we worked so hard for our whole young lives, are put on hold and slowly we put on a couple of extra pounds.

While we may never forget how to ride a bike, doing tricks on the handlebars or riding wheelies, for instance, become a thing of the past without room to keep up on these old practice-makes-perfect abilities. Sometimes this can be a devastating blow to the psyche; Ask any gymnast, magician, or writer. Some things you have to do everyday or you sit and watch as the hands of time slowly backpedal all of your progress. But this is what life is all about isn't it? Eventually taking joy in watching your kids find enjoyment in the activities you once *lived* for? A soft yes is the answer. The problem arises when focus falls from the positive outcome of the life you began as that hobbyist, to the negative outcome you see in losing all of that practice time. Too often, those of us who draw in a few degrees during this transition, don't ever seem to open back up.

Solitude is an invisible foe. Once we begin to feel that we don't have a passion to offer others, we seldom try to make meaningful connections in the community. No interest lies in meeting and mingling with people of a job you work only to pay the bills, much less with folks from church where you may not be able to have a drink. Eventually the excitement of life becomes foreign to us and we turn to some substance to liven us back up or add extra hours to our days. Then it is no wonder we chalk up addictions or habits to the simplistic excuse of, "I just like the way it makes me feel!"

A lot of addicts have no problem identifying in this way. Drugs like crack, pain killers, and disaccosiatives are the worst in this regard. They're made to feel good. Of course, the recovery feels horrible, but during our high or habit we'll literally feel like a kid again. Interest, energy, and excitement; the whole nine yards. If the hangover and losses aren't enough to make someone quit, then what is? How do you put a thing like that down?

Often enough people stay on those types of drugs for so long, that the withdrawal is actually deadly. Even alcohol can kill you after a really long bender and cold turkey quitting. Substances like these are a double edged sword. The withdrawal from even a day on these drugs can be so bad that sometimes the user just continues on use the next morning to prevent from feeling that downward withdrawal or showing discontent in front of family and friends. Ups and downs are tale-tell signs of mental issues and addicts know this. If an addict gets stuck in a situation where they must work, or carry out duties days at a time, they may keep taking a substance just to make it to a lull in activity where they can sleep for a couple of days to recover. If they go too long, the tremors can be deadly if not treated with benzodiazipines soon enough. There are protocols at hospitals to actually administer the worst alcoholics beer while they dry up in ICU in order to keep them alive.

Even if someone manages to put down a drug that makes them feel that way, then how is it ever possible to keep them away from going back to it? This is a fear that many users are familiar with. It is something so strong that some even feel as if they were on their death bed, just a single use of their secret substance may revive them all together. It is common to hear in substance abuse circles, "When I quit is when I'll die." or "Addiction is what keeps me young." What evidence do we have to the contrary?

It has been proven that substances which have no addictive properties can be just as addicting to a person's brain as those which are naturally habit forming. Meaning that addiction is a thing of the mind. What was found was that synapses in the brain create neural pathways between thought, action, sense, and emotion. Feeling young again, brings back all the enthusiasm of a whole life ahead of you. A time when inhibitions were just a mystery to us. The energy, painlessness, careless, excitability, or euphoria that an individual associates most with their childhood

The Only Thing I Like About Living

can be directly connected to the simple action, taste, or sensation which comes with ingesting a particular substance; even a certain food. Furthermore, not all of these attributes of youth need be present, only one will do. Each individual associates more strongly with each of these traits. Just as everyone sometimes gets a passing scent that reminds them of a favorite memory, we also gets passing *feelings* the same way. Imagine if you could find the source of those elusive scents you sometimes get an inkling of but can never pinpoint. If we could get a hold of those things and bottle them up, there would be many people who would sleep with the bottle curled up to their chests forever more. Like a living memory, feelings associated with youth can be the hardest things to let go of.

So what are we to do?

3

When we unravel the mystery of our addictions, we can start healing. The truth is, those feelings we remember, are not natural. Not anymore. We aren't those kids anymore. We are adults. Even younger men and women, who have suffered with addiction, are adults, in substance abuse, because they have experienced their loss over and over again. Not just physical loss that comes with the damage of careless spending, and selfish action which fulfills our needs. I'm talking about the actual loss. The actual loss I am referring to is the loss of the memory of our childhood over and over again. Losing a child is said to be the worst human experience in the known palette of sentience. When someone loses themselves, it can rival even that feeling.

That kid we loved to be, those dreams we thought were possible, that drive we possessed to be the best. That kid died every time the drug wore off. Trauma causes age, physical or emotional. Yes, addicts are adults that never could leave the kid but instead watched them die over and over again. But feeling like that kid doesn't bring them back. We are different now. We have different feelings now that we're older. The huge growth of exponential discovery has passed, now only small discoveries lie ahead and the big ones will be far between. We are better. We are bigger. Most of all, discipline now pays off in even bigger dividends.

The true reason it is so alluring to relive the experience of being young is because when we were young everything in our personal world was going in an acceptable direction. Even if our life sucked as a child. Even those of us who were abused, mistreated, or brought up in poverty; our lives were going in an acceptable direction as far as our soul was concerned. Everything that was happening back then was not our fault- We were kids. There was no accountability for our actions besides a swat on the ass, disappointment, or grounding. Maybe even a little jail time as teens was not enough to make us accountable for our actions. We were young, still learning, still innocent. When do we become accountable?

The answer is now. We are always going to be someone's little boy or girl, but that doesn't mean we never have to be an adult. Growing up is scary but pretending that we will

The Only Thing I Like About Living

never have to be accountable for our actions is not the answer. When you're addicted to something, anything, you're disguising your fear of looking forward and being part of that experience indefinitely. We are acting out the child's tantrum in pantomime.

"I don't wanna! I don't wanna! No!"

Kicking and screaming we've been having the world drag us into adulthood; The trap we never wanted to fall victim to. You see, we love the feeling of unaccountability because or soul remains so clean, which lets our minds believe that we're headed straight through the pearly gates in the end (or wherever pleasant place you believe the good natured go to). When we're finally being passed the baton, when it comes to the ownership and responsibility of where our soul is headed, some of us find a new high gear to step up our pace, right at the last moment. We attempt to outrun our teammate for a while longer and will even hit the nitro if they get too close. But were just exhausting our team, and when we finally decide to take the baton, we're gonna have to dig much deeper to make it the last few steps ourselves since we already overdid it.

It is time to take the baton.

Don't be afraid, don't be hasty, and don't do anything drastic. All those things are gonna happen, or have happened, when we decide to do it. They will happen on their own. Taking responsibility for our souls direction is one the most rewarding things you can ever do. It is, in fact, why adults like being adults. You did know that some adults actually enjoy being grown-up didn't you? Well, it's true. Just because we may have grown up in a family who was sarcastic, underpaid, overworked, and overstressed doesn't mean that other adults out there don't love living their lives. We once may have even wanted to become one. Successful people, well, the happy ones anyhow, have one thing in common, they know what we knew as kids; that everything is going in an acceptable direction. The only difference is, adults are responsible, accountable, and proud of it. Your soul is yours. Own it.

Jay Horne

BOREDOM

The Only Thing I Like About Living

Jay Horne

1

If you are like me and unable to enjoy your periods of serenity, feeding the spirit is the one thing that can fill idle time without causing harm. We all know what idle hands lead to.

It is important to have a place where you can practice your spirituality. There are two different practitioners of spirit. Those who need a place of solitude to practice and those who seek out a congregation of peers.

I am an extreme example of someone who cannot live without a isolated haven to be with my spirit. My wife, on the other hand, is a homemaker and she spends two whole days a week taking our four kids to her huge church in which all of our children take part in some part of a program or volunteer service. My wife is satisfied with a congregation. She belongs to Jesus and Me, in that order.

I am not satisfied with a man speaking in front of a congregation. While I can receive pieces of the sermon and integrate them into my beliefs, attending this service and reading a bible doesn't fill me up with any feeling of achievement when it comes to my spirituality. I like to think of myself as more of a mystic. While I don't fall into the conspiracy trap of overboard theorists, I have seen some unexplainable things in my life and my family's history that have proven to me through experience that my part to play in the spiritual world is more active. A few psychic premonitions, and some strange interconnected coincidences throughout my studies of different hobbies have led me down a different path to the divine. Without time to practice martial arts, and devote some of my time actively assembling spiritual power through intentional physical activities, I don't feel I have been growing in my convictions.

We all need to find for ourselves what our convictions are attuned with and then attempt to set up a way that makes us feel good about furthering them. Reading, praying, teaching, hiking, meditating, joining a church, and attending study groups or AA meetings, are some ideas. But all of these things aren't going to fill up the entire space of our down times. Some of us also need a hobby and exercise. Most importantly, we need to understand why boredom becomes a larger entity when we age and use that understanding to better enjoy our brief moments of pure relaxation.

We have worked hard for our times of serenity and, as adults, sometimes falsely identify these moments as boredom. When we take on the responsibility of adulthood we grow more cautiously aware of the dangers of the mischief we enjoyed so much as children. Our kids take on interests, and our time able to spend on our own grows narrow.

Any gymnast, magician, or professional athlete, can tell you that their inability to practice their passion daily can be heart wrenching. What once was a dream of being the best in their field, only achievable through monstrous dedication, becomes distant and impossible. These losses can deal a heavy blow to the psyche, and create a deep sense of pointlessness in training at all. Of course, the stagnant nature of those of us who were so involved in such passions, during our youth, will lead to anxiety and boredom as parents.

This anxiety and boredom often turns to drinking or other unhealthy habits in order to actively unhinge that scale that grows too balanced in us who are use to constant growth. How do we stipend these feelings and thoughts?

In Eastern Mysticism, the Buddhist monk meets his unity with God through the practice of thoughtlessness. Many philosophies believe that the purpose of thought is a process whereby the need for thought is slowly removed over a long period of evolution. Every person goes throughout their day, whether it be at work, or in the gym, repeating actions involving thought, deduction, and ultimately effort. With time, those actions become easier, and sometimes even boring. Our action can border on autonomous without a conscious effort to modify the regimen or make it more challenging. Unfortunately we sometimes attempt to do this through negative habits. Is your daily regimen necessarily healthy, or beneficial?

2

Even when we are leading a more fulfilling and mentally healthy lifestyle, we can't stay active and moving about twenty four hours a day. Thinking like that will lead us to other addictive habits like funneling down five energy drinks a day or seeking therapy and medication on a false pretense of never having enough energy. It would be exhausting to try and achieve a schedule where you are cramming in family time, exercise, spiritual practice, hobbies, and work or school. Sometimes just work and family time is overly exhausting itself!

A man I once worked with on an ambulance had once been a pro-wrestler. He had spent his entire life living on pain killers and competing in the ring, like many of those guys do. When he finally succumbed to a career ending injury he had to seek help to break his addiction to the narcotics. After his success and finding a new job, it wasn't long before he began working extreme hours and spending less time with his wife and kids. Finally when his family came to a breaking point, due to his frequent absence, he looked at his history and determined he had moved his addictive action to another area of his life. He had become a workaholic.

Being an addict is exhausting for everyone involved! We can't go from exhausting ourselves and others through our preference of alcohol and drugs over people, right to preferring our work or hobbies over them instead. Our lives have to have *some* balance. Besides that, we deserve to be able to relax.

The thought of myself deserving anything was a huge barrier for me. That, in part, was a major reason I found myself so busy all of the time. If we're busy, we can't confront our true feelings about ourselves. It's our feelings that allow or disallow us to enjoy our peace. This is where we start to explore the three ingredients of freedom.

Peace is understandably one of the main ingredients in being free of boredom, addiction, and solitude. It is the center post in nearly ever religious following around the globe. Obtaining peace is, in some instances, the sole aim of spiritual practices. Eastern Buddhism, Taoism, meditative disciplines, and even the fictional order of the Jedi from Lucasfilms, orbit the idea of peace being freedom to directly connect with the spirit. A

The Only Thing I Like About Living

calm mind, not occupied by the busyness of excess thought and emotion, is what the term refers to, but the definitive meaning of peace is actually '*freedom* from disturbance'.

Here, I am speaking about freedom in everything. Freedom in finances, freedom from addictions, freedom from habits, freedom from anxiety, and freedom from uncertainty. Removing these disturbances, emotionally, brings us the freedom to be who it is, what we want to be, and the ability to feel happy about it.

Freedom is not at all real freedom if you are unhappy. No one is happy about things they do not want to do, or are they? Peace cannot be obtained while actively seeking *happiness*. Because we are at conscious work while still attempting to claim this second essential ingredient, it is important we discuss *happiness* to ensure we end up with a complete experience of freedom.

The last ingredient is *intention*. *Intentions* are kind of the last few steps of the AA twelve step program; the part of the program where you maintain your freedom, which consists of *peace* and *happiness*. All the while the third ingredient, *intention*, brings you the things that will make you happy before you ever even need request them, thus reciprocating the *peace* and *happiness* in your daily life.

PEACE & SERENITY

The Only Thing I Like About Living

1

It took me almost two months to pick up my white chip during my meetings again. I had been sober the whole time, but the blooms on that vine I spoke of earlier hadn't yet begun to open on my understanding of what I was up to until then. Though I had quit drinking, my family was back together, and things were even keel again, I still didn't feel that I had started making a change yet. I was, in a lot of ways, faking it. You can know that you've made the conviction to leave alcohol forever and still feel like the only thing you like about being alive is drinking.

What made me feel like I was ready to take that chip was when I finally felt that I was taking the first step on my path to freedom. Ultimately, by the end of that meeting I had a good comprehension of what the first ingredient was on the path to that freedom. Though I may not have yet been happy, which later I would find out was another ingredient in the process, I discovered what it meant to be serene.

The very room we met in was called the serenity room and for five years the serenity prayer had sat in my pocket as part of my key chain. It is a simple prayer that opens each meeting at AA.

God grant me the serenity to accept the things I cannot change, the courage to change the things I can, and the wisdom to know the difference.

I, like many addicts, found myself trading addictions out for other ones. Drinking a gallon of tea a day, smoking, even running insane distances. There was no enjoyment in just sitting still; no quieting the soul as it begged for that imbalance and movement. I just wanted change. I couldn't get enough of change.

That day a senior recovering addict explained how she felt useless in the nearing death of her elderly mother, because she didn't know precisely what she could do to help her. Her inability to help was driving her to want a drink because something inside of her wanted to move. Some spirit in her wanted change, whether it be a helpful growing change in the eyes of her family or a hopeless decaying change in the light of her drinking.

In another instance a woman broke her sobriety of four years one night when she was faced with making a tough decision. Her inability to choose a path to her future, whether it be leaving a husband or quitting her job, or pulling the plug on a relative's life-support; drove her to drink in hopes of making the decision easier. It didn't help her, instead it made matters worse, the decision was still never made, and now she sat among her peers crying and relapsing.

Most alcoholics and addicts can't have *a day* of weakness and return to sobriety the following day. After a drink or a drug, many addicts go on another bender straight back to bottom. It's the allure of that ever present desire for movement.

A man once said that he quit drinking three times in his life. The first was as a teenager when his mom found him naked in his own barf one morning and he quit through embarrassment. The second was when he took a self-inventory and realized that all of his co-workers of ten years had nice homes, kids in college, and nice cars; yet he had a unkempt yard and a beat up motorcycle making the same wages- he quit that time because he felt he had been working for nothing. The third time he quit, which was the worst, may have never had to happen had he not said to himself, four months after his second time quitting, "You're doing good. You have punished yourself enough." That time he quit from jail. He finished his story by telling us that he was never so happy and grateful for his simple freedom and home, and that was when he finally understood the old saying "*A grateful sober man will find it easy to remain one.*"

Rewards. That drink, that extra narcotic, that cigarette, that chocolate, that scratch-off ticket, all things that we addicts look at as a regular person's right, is not a reward. They can never be. What have they ever rewarded us with? They are all simply an allure to that ever present need for change, and the over active empathy to the ebb and flow of the universe that some of us possess.

When I see the serenity prayer now, I understand why we are requesting serenity to accept the things we cannot change. Because, it is always the one day that we think we need to change something, whether for the better or worse that *will* drive us to a pointless or stupid decision. That woman who relapsed for a day thought that one day of drinking again (of stopping punishing herself) would 'do it' for her. But what she really needed was a day of serenity. It is okay to have weak days, those days you should take serenity in, and allow yourself to accept that you cannot change anything at all.

Some of us have an ever-present awareness of the threat of death bearing down on us from the future. The eventuality of it causes us to feel that a single day of serenity is a waste of our precious time here. Would I be wrong to assume this is a false statement? It is an exercise in perception. We fail to see that each day we expend our energy we are suppose to be climbing closer to a place of rest. Rest is the gift. When we fall victim to our anxiety, because of a fear of growing away from the young vitality of our childhood, we end up spending energy on needless activity and pointless habits. Those habits lead to chaos, generated haphazardly through our impatience, and we gladly welcome them back time and time again to ease our painstakingly earned stints of boredom. It's like burning money.

The Only Thing I Like About Living

Jay Horne

HAPPINESS

The Only Thing I Like About Living

1

I once termed Heaven as 'My life relived minus all of the bad choices'. After all of these years, I don't think I was far off with the definition. When I look back at the things that have occurred throughout my life, it is sometimes hard to determine the exact point at which I made a wrong decision, leading into the postponing of an easy going and positive lifestyle. Sometimes the decisions are so elusive they disguise themselves as not a choice at all. The real truth is that sometimes not making a seemingly difficult choice can be the wrong choice. Who says Heaven can't sometimes be difficult? If you had made that difficult choice, perhaps the bad would have never come to pass. Then that difficult choice would simply be a part of your Heaven experience. Would Heaven get boring if there were never any choices?

I like to think that Sin is the roadblock to Happiness, because sin stacks up. What I mean is that good deeds never have a tendency to stack or compile. We don't come to the end of two months of good doing and say, "Okay Lord, I would like to cash in!" The benefits come of their own accord, and blessing is bestowed as we go. This is why we can have a great relationship with someone for years, and then one mistake can ruin the whole thing. No one ever looks back and says, "My husband took care of me and my children for twenty years... another nineteen years of cheating on me with that woman and it's over!"

In many cases, if we consider the good deeds we have done for someone, or the good way we have treated someone as sacrifices that we have made, we may miss an opportunity for reconciliation. Goodness is never a sacrifice. The sacrifice is in the single sin. Sin, and the sacrifices that come with it, on the other hand, stack up in a saving s account. When we come to the end of a long bout of sinning we always wind up on our knees saying, "Please Lord! I am ready to cash in. Forgive me!" ... and then of course, Jesus forgives us of our sins in our sincerity and off we go to start saving up again. Sin is, in fact, causing chaos all along. It just gets worse and worse until we easily notice it, and then so bad we can no longer bare it. People survive sin for really long times. It's only when humanity reaches a precipice that we ever really want to change, and that has a lot to do with faith.

Whether people label it or not, faith is what helps us to make the right decision all of the time. If we knew that nothing bad would happen because of a choice that we made, that we would sustain no losses; If we knew that we would not be outdone or showed up, or would not be proven wrong, would we ever not make the right choice, the good choice, the choice that the angel side of the shoulders pulls us to? Ego is what allures us to make a wrong decision in fear of someone else (without a conscience) taking the easy road and getting ahead.

So what does a good choice look like? How is a decision, or a non-decision deemed right, and good, and true, under God? Guidelines for positive choice are laid out in biblical scripture, but if you look at the underlying reasons for our decisions, and weight them against what a Godly person may decide, things become clear. The success of the WWJD 'What would Jesus do?' campaign of the late 1990's was based loosely on this concept.

For example: Take the misconception of time; The book of Job speaks of the faults inherent of a life of riches. One who is wealthy can be born into riches, play fun games, grow up spending money, have their buckets always full of milk ... and yet never know the pleasure of a meal. They go through life only to die and miss out on all the things that they should be thankful for because they never were taught the gospel of the Lord. It is eluded to that the grave may only be found because of ignorance and or a lack of interest in the divine.

Job 21 13 They spend their days in wealth, and in a moment go down to the grave. Job 21 26 They shall lie down alike in the dust, and the worms shall cover them.

If a person has worked diligently for many years to attain a wealth of savings for a special trip and two days before the trip an expensive opportunity arises to help someone in the name of the Lord—do you not help the person? Through the scripture, it becomes clear that the withholding of such help would actually hasten a grave. To give freely, outside of the limiting confines of time, would be blessing. Why would the good man choose to withhold his blessing, if the fear of time existed not? The man of faith is aware that the Lord gives him life everlasting. A trip the man has waited patiently for is hardly something that cannot again be saved for.

Proverbs 23 5 Wilt thou set thine eyes on that which is not? Riches make themselves wings and fly away as an eagle toward Heaven.

All of this sets of alarms in our brains. Statements like, "Oh how great it would be to be able to give like that!"

The point is, we will never be able until after we give like that. Great fear fills the mind of those who harbor doubt through their own sin. We are all guilty of it in our own degrees.

Religious dedication is not something that is necessary to cultivate happiness. I use examples from the King James Bible because it is the most recognizable piece of literature on the planet. What is really key in harnessing lasting happiness is the ability to foresee a future where we can be actively and thankfully involved. This is harder than it sounds. Just as we stated earlier when we challenged ourselves to take the baton, our accountability for our own soul is the only thing that will allow us to purge ourselves of the sin that blocks our positive outlook on the future. Only then can we effectively use the most powerful tool we own to manifest the happiness that brings peace. That tool is thankfulness.

The Only Thing I Like About Living

2

Many addicts and alcoholics claim that their road to recovery came in some super intense flash of intuition or experience that totally rewired their way of thinking. They call it their enlightenment or Ah Ha moment.

Mine was back in 2005 while I was studying auras and Kundalini. I was working at a Waffle House at the time, and it actually came in three parts. The strongest, and longest lasting of which was a sense of total loss of the self. I experienced it as a great big crunch that, for all conscious memory resulted in essentially, death. The enormous sense of doom leading to the crunch was followed by an explosion of light that took my soul with it along a ladder of infinite experience I can only explain as pure energy.

It was as if I sat at the throne of the distributor and during my time there I could clearly see that I was born to this Earth with a purpose, to be fulfilled only by the knowledge of my own destiny. The image before me was one of Utopia and a worry free, autonomous existence; One in which everyone spoke continually of the goodness and glory of God and unity. Revealed to me through that absence of self was a world, much like the one we inhabit now but with a people who remind one another that every moment is a gift from God, predetermined in a past we can not conceive of, as it is attached to a future abstractly absolute.

These enlightening moments of my life were always followed by a period of lingering satisfaction as days turned to weeks and reality slowly returned. I truly was not yet living in that future, but instead inhabited the present where differences still prevailed. I knew that I was destined for Utopia, but I would have to live through the present where much growth still needed to be achieved. For weeks after my final episode, I was incredibly thankful. I was thankful to have been put back here so graciously to fulfill my vision, thankful for my positive future, and thankful I wasn't stuck in that expanse, conscious of the extreme sacrifice that the creator is always undergoing. But, as time went on my thankfulness gradually faded. If I am honest with myself, I think it is because I became so comfortable with the fact that my future was ensured that I again took up sin. I have no doubt, and I can see that sin, is the roadblock to happiness and also that thankfulness is the shortcut to it.

I am often asked, especially by those who don't believe in a creator, or those who don't think there is anyone listening, who we should be thankful too? I was thankful to myself, in a strange way, for surviving the ordeal. I sometimes think that if I had not been practicing Kundalini at the time, the foreign feeling of what happened to me may well have destroyed me. But, be thankful to your own God, or if you are agnostic or atheist, be thankful to a future version of you. A version of you that you have, or once had, as an old wise person, or successful person, or simply a happy, peaceful person. Why is it important to be thankful? The answer is simple. Because thankfulness leaves no room for negative energy.

What is negative energy? What is energy?

I like to say that there are three types of people in this world. The ones who know, the ones who don't know, and the ones who think they know. If someone knows, beyond all shadow of doubt that their beliefs are true, then they have proven their theories through their own time and experiences. If someone doesn't know, they are aware that they have yet to confirm their intuitions about belief, and are waiting for that experience that solidifies it. Those who think they know, have a great understanding of beliefs in, or not in, something, but have not experienced an event to prove to them that what they believe is true but are convicted to never stray from that theology for the sake of their soul which they may have a theoretical but not an experiential understanding, as of yet.

No matter which kind of person you are, the concept of energy is easily understand with a basic concept of science. Things move, and the movement creates energy, kinetically. This energy can be transferred to another object like a marble, and expended in whatever outlet possible. Be it through movement, heat, or other actions the energy transforms. It is known that energy can neither be created or destroyed. It simply changes form.

Even for an individual who believes that the entire universe is just some fabrication, it can be reasonably argued that things are moving. Time continues no matter what you attempt. Despite if the universe exists on a trillion leaflets of film that our

The Only Thing I Like About Living

souls transgress to make a moving history or experience in senses; the scene still changes. The pages still flip. The blip of our soul goes from one to another, no?

So we can assume at its most basic level of understanding, at least there is some kind of movement. With this movement there will be energy that can be changed.

[Neale Donald Walsh](#) called this movement of energy emotion. As in e-motion, energy in motion. I like to agree with it, because it makes it easier to show why thankfulness is important.

3

There was once an experiment done by some Taoist priests in which they were asked to meditate or pray over some petri dishes of water. The experiment was to show how water has the unusual ability to carry the effect of medications though it had been diluted a trillion times, because of an effect called the placebo effect. Most of us know the placebo effect as the method of how they determine if medication works or not by administering two patients of the same controls different liquids. One patient gets the normal water, and the other the medicine. Then they study how much the patient reacts to the medication as opposed to the patient who just thought he got the medication but actually ingested water.

Well, this experiment is called such, because before this became a common practice, doctors were baffled on how patients were recovering after medication shortages where the patients were getting doses that had been diluted to thousandths of a percent of their normal strengths in order to not cause panic. They were finding pure water, simply poured from the same vials where medication was stored could have the same effect as the original medication. It was as if the water was remembering the makeup of the liquid.

Anyhow, these Taoist priests were each placed in a room alone with a petri dish of water and asked to send different meditative thoughts to these dishes. One was happiness, another was, anger, and another love, thankfulness, greed, etc. Then the dishes were placed in a freezer and the resulting ice crystals were documented and put on display at an art exhibit. The results were inarguable. The dishes that had been positively energized through love, happiness, and thankfulness became beautiful patterns resembling intricate snowflakes, while the negatively charged petri dishes failed to grow discerning patterns. It is interesting to look at, as you can see that the negative dishes seemed congealed or stifled, beside the others who radiated and expanded in all directions.

Thankfulness is not one of the three ingredients that bring freedom, but it is an imperative part of the third ingredient which is *intention*.

The Only Thing I Like About Living

Jay Horne

INTENTION

The Only Thing I Like About Living

1

The last ingredient is *intention*. *Intentions* are kind of the last few steps of the AA twelve step program; the part of the program where you maintain your freedom, which consists of *peace* and *happiness*. All the while the third ingredient, *intention*, brings you the things that will make you happy before you ever even need request them, thus reciprocating the *peace* and *happiness* in your daily life

Breaking it down into its most basic terminology, the maintenance of a clean spirit comes down to two things. Continually inventorying our conscience and promptly admitting wrong doing when it happens. On the other hand, staying aligned with righteousness will not be easy unless you stay aware of your intentions from dawn to dusk. After we further discuss addictions, I will lay out three steps that will help anyone and everyone keep that in focus throughout the day.

We all know that life is not perfect, but that doesn't stop cultures like the Japanese and Chinese trying to perfect it. Feng Shui, for example, or even western interior decorating. And what else would life be for, than to attempt to perfect it?

I almost titled this book, "The Power of a Clean Conscience", because once you get real about where it is we want to be in the future, we can really start to make choices based on that desire. The importance behind knowingly being deserving of all of the happiness we wish for cannot be stressed enough. It is in a clean conscience that we will find comfort in the hardships that we face along the path to our future.

When we face conflict along our path in life, it easy to bless the misfortune as part of the greater plan when we are sure that we do not deserve a negative penance. During AA's twelve step program there is a step that guides us through reaching out to all of those we have done wrong to and make amends. I'm not saying that such an extreme is necessarily vital. But, to some, it may be.

The concept of washing ourselves clean of wrongdoing is an important practice. It's why baptisms take place everyday. Personally, I use Jesus for this crucial step in developing my inner peace and happiness.

The Only Thing I Like About Living

My reasons for this are due to my spiritual understandings. Every person has different beliefs, and indeed, it should be that way. If it was an age before the time of Christ, I would undoubtedly wash myself of sin by swimming in the ocean or other natural body of water. This I still do, and even still symbolically so. Yet, some people find it necessary to seek out every person they have ever done wrong in order to purge themselves. For others, it is as easy as a proclamation, awakening to a new day, or the sacrifice of a habit or pleasure.

The main premise in purging, is the ability it opens up to move forward. When the purge is complete or dedicated to, only then can we undertake the huge responsibility of keeping our souls or conscience clean.

Just as when we were young children and acted innocently, unable to sour our will or happiness, we can act now. We will revel in the light-footed experiences we encounter, and additionally take pride in the accountability of such freedom as adults. We will own our lifestyle. And we will do this by having pure intent on where it is we are headed.

What about the woman whose just found lung cancer? What about the man who decides to do these things and have intent, but gets arrested for his past wrong doings a day later? When is it too late to try? No single thing on this planet would ever have been attempted if all the possible objections had to first been overcome.

An archer can get really good at putting an arrow onto the his string, drawing the bow, and releasing the shot, but until he starts aiming at something he will never hit his intended target. Not even by accident, because his only intent has ever been to shoot.

Peter Pan says, "Death is the next great adventure!" and Captain Hook says, "Death is the only adventure."
Let us want for genuine goodness.
I ask you,
What are the few brief years of life, to the task of perfecting the soul?

Jay Horne

ADDICTION

The Only Thing I Like About Living

Jay Horne

1

Everything is potentially addictive. We can become unfocused and lose our ability to apply intention when we feel that we are entitled to any one thing. Sometimes that other guy is going to have everything we desire, but we can never know what that person has or is or will eventually sacrifice to hold it as we stand watching. Being entitled to anything is something, we as adults, have learned is simply smoke in a headlamp, a mirror in the desert, or water in a fist. It should not be grasped at. We all think we deserve things for different reasons.

"I've been sober for over a year! I deserve this!" says one.

"Who cares! I've been sober my whole life!" says the other.

Entitlement is an illusion. I venture to say again that no one has ever achieved a thing in this world alone. It is only as possible to pay all of our dues as it is to be entitled to payment. Do we expect our children to repay us for conceiving them?

Why does the singularity of one simple noun, contain so much magnetic allure for some us? Each of us are unique, and because of it, we all have a *thing*. That thing, that one thing, was put as a challenge to Mitch by Curly, in a Hollywood film starring Billy Crystal called City Slickers, back in the 90's.

This old cowboy put a finger up in the air and said, "You know what the secret to life is? This."

"Your finger?" Mitch asked.

"Nope. One thing. Just one thing." Curly said as he shifted his hand-rolled cigarette from one corner of his mouth to the other.

"What thing?"

"That, is for you to figure out." He said with a grin.

Train your focus on something, but don't feel entitled to it. I have learned that the one thing I can always rely on to be there is the image I have for myself in the distant future. I have grown to see that picture of myself, which I have fashioned in my mind, as a sort of guardian angel. Maybe it is, in fact, my Guardian Angel. My faults, my decisions, my strengths, my power to forgive, my accountability, my hope, my hobbies, my

The Only Thing I Like About Living

family ... everything, is thanks to that vision of myself. What lies beyond that vision, I can not know until I make it there.

All of us, when it comes down to the most basic logic, love our vices because of the way they are going to make us feel. When we get a hold of them they drive us until we run out of gas and watch us make our way walking back to town from the muddy dead end they let us out at. It's great while we can pay. As adults, we run out of gas faster. There is an old saying—

You can't turn a pickle back into a cucumber.

Sometimes, we step in puddles. That's life. I heard, recently that life is not to be endured, but rather to be enjoyed. Enjoyment can only come from selflessness that eventually reciprocates itself through unintentional and unmotivated reception of gratitude. Let us decide to shift our focus from the one thing we feel entitled too, to the one thing we knew we should grow up to be as children. Only then, when we find ourselves in muddy puddles, will we remember to splash.

Jay Horne

OVERCOME

The Only Thing I Like About Living

Jay Horne

1

As you journey into the beyond with your new knowledge and understanding, find peers. Your current place in the universe will always remain the same without some kind of action. Creation wants to fill the canvas of your life with all of the images you can imagine for yourself, but it can't paint a multitude with only one color.

People and their experience's are the palette. Even if you can only manage to drag yourself into a meeting of a bunch of old drunks, and sit there in silence everyday—do that!

As I sat in a meeting, with those drunks, one of them said, "You know, I never believed in anything but I was always successful because I would find the guy at my job making the most money and ask how he did it. Then I would do what he did the best I could." he leaned back and crossed his arms, "People always want to tell you what they believe because they want to think that they know some kind of secret, but I always just do what the guy does, minus the mumbo jumbo." he said.

"I didn't know how to quit drinking and fix my life," he shook his head, grinning like he couldn't believe what he was saying, "but I saw a couple guys in AA that had done just that… So I asked." he said.

"The man I asked told me exactly what he does everyday, and I started doing it, just like that. I didn't have to believe a damn thing, never did.

"I got up in the morning and prayed to stay away from a drink. During the day when I had a chance or thought to drink, I prayed to have strength to say no. At night, I said a prayer of thanks for making it through the day without a drink—

that was 32 years ago. I still take it one day at a time. Sometimes one hour at a time." the man leaned forward over the table, his hands a pyramid, fingers dancing together, "Sometimes I hear people say, 'You want a better life? Just quit drinking! Simple as that! Never touch the stuff again, no matter what!', and I think to myself, 'Well, that's just what I did.' and you know what? Everything they promised me that would happen when I quit, came true."

The Only Thing I Like About Living

Jay Horne

THE PROMISES

The Only Thing I Like About Living

1

In the beginning, God created Man in his likeness and the Heaven and the Earth as Mans' dominion; an existence of peace, beauty, and of everlasting life. We all know that man eventually disobeyed God by eating the fruit of knowledge of good and evil which brought difficulty to his existence, but have we ever asked why God gave us such a gift to begin with? It is written in Galatians 3:22 that the promise of Jesus Christ be given to those that believe. The promise of Jesus Christ is for everlasting life and a return to the goodness and peace of the Garden for which we were created.

I have often heard in service that the temptation of sin can be more easily staved off if the potential sinner focus on the *promise* of the Lord. The temporary pleasure of sin holds no measure to the abundant reward and promise. What is temporary ecstasy to an infinite existence of chaos free life?

When Adam and Eve partook of the fruit, they were essentially devaluing the promise of God. For God promised them dominion and joy to multiply, and the tree of life; "Only do not eat from the one tree of knowledge".

The same that was true in the beginning is again true after the sacrifice of his only son, Jesus Christ. God has a *promise* for everyone. The promise is that you are to inherit his Kingdom. You shall live easy, and free, and multiply if you have faith and show goodness. Why does he promise us this? Why did he promise Adam and Eve the same, in the beginning? The simple answer is, "He had no choice."

Before the firmament was formed and before God created the likeness of himself on Earth, he was alone in the void with only his magnificent self. To give us existence was to pattern his self-realization. God knew, upon the creation of his likeness, that nothing was needed for his people to sit beside him in his power and glory, but faith. For he was in the beyond and knew that it was good. His natural promise was that his experiential existence was inevitable, for he began as the end that was definite. His offspring had no choice but to become as he through faith, less they try and go their own way. The way to God was in doing nothing but what already had been done, procreating, for God had existed before the firmament. It is in deviating from faith that chaos is introduce in life. Remember the promise to abate Sin.

Faith, in no way, is exclusive to religious sects. Faith is simply complete trust or confidence in something. If we are lacking faith, it is an internal conflict between what we are doing and where it is we think we are going. Once we learn to clarify the destination we are trying to get to, and combine that with aligning our actions to reflect that future, faith blossoms and becomes unbreakable.

Faith is what makes the promises of a better life through better understanding and practice possible to guarantee. When there is no reason in your mind that something bad should happen to you, no negative karma following you around, when a difficult event arises it is easy to see the big picture through your faith.

2

Alcoholics Anonymous also has promises. For some they are the driving force behind their endeavor to complete the program. The promises of sobriety guarantee that we will be amazed halfway through when we become free and happy. Isn't that an awesome, down-to-earth promise? Before we even know it, we will be free and happy. That is the very first promise. The next is that we will no longer regret our past and we will gain peace through an understanding of serenity. Selfishness will become as foreign as sobriety once was and people will become interesting. Then situations, like chaos, which used to baffle us, will become easily manageable.

These promises aren't all that extravagant. They are things that normal people actually feel and experience throughout their lives.

Sometimes I can attend a whole meeting and hear nothing but people complaining about everyday life. Those meetings are not a waste of time for me, they make me smile and appreciate the little annoyances that life is sometimes filled with as compared to the huge worries that come with addiction.

One guy was saying that he really started understanding how invaluable his life had become when he was a week sober. Hearing the frame of his bed squeak, as got in and out nightly was driving him nuts. He had once halfheartedly repaired it when his fiancée had told him months earlier that it woke her every time he came home late. Being sober now, he was making another attempt at it and had spent an hour this day taking the frame apart and fixing it right. He told us that he spent his morning bitching about all the tools he needed and the running to the store he had to do, but eventually he had got it done *correctly*. This time, he wasn't slapping the damn thing together, any which way he could, in order to get back to drinking; he was really fixing it. I could tell by the brief look on his face that he was ashamed of himself for all the years that he shortchanged his fiancée by letting the selfishness of drinking change his outlook on time. Sober now, he was thankful that his fiancée was still around and chuckled saying, "These are the things I worry about now. Changing the light bulbs, fixing the bed frame; not the police suddenly kicking down my door or something. What a relief!".

The promise of undertaking a positive change in lifestyle and freeing yourself from stubborn addictions, is simply that life will get better. That subconscious worry will stop stunting your spiritual and social growth. The promises come of their own accord and sometimes surprise us. My promise to you that this stuff works, is just the same.

Better yet—you don't need to believe. It will make a believer out of you.

Jay Horne

THE STEPS

The Only Thing I Like About Living

1

It comes down to us. What would be easier than copying over the 12 step program from the big blue book? I have always been an instant gratification kind of guy, and like many addicts and habit-forming prone individuals, I wished there was a three step program. So here it is.

The most important part of a life changing habit is to form it. Differing research will tell you that it will take anything from twenty one days to one thousand repetitions to form a habit. Opinions are just as abundant as the assholes who share them, and they all stink—or something like that. The main thing is to practice these three simple steps every single day.

If we were to follow the blue book's recommendation and start by admitting we have a problem and deciding to hand it over to a higher power we would get the same results. In our daily practice, let's remain actively aware our intention and our faults will stay away. We can't fail to believe in a higher power when a substance claimed that seat already by controlling our emotions. There is always something stronger than us, even if it only exists out there in the future. Try and stop time. Even if you succeed, it always starts ticking again, eventually.

The Only Thing I Like About Living

STEP ONE

When you wake up, get on your knees right by where you laid your head last night and think of the old man or woman you one day would like to be (all of his attributes, his or her accomplishments, the things that your grandchildren, friends, or random person seeking an old hermit, might come and seek you out for). Will they come seek you for advice, money, friendship, or simply just to awe at your beauty? Don't want to live to be old? Well then think of the young super star you would like to be that may elude you by a meager ten years or so. Think of yourself happy. Be snow skiing or hiking, or be with family and friends in comfort. If you have a hard time picturing any of this, or don't yet know for what you want to be sought after, then refer back to memories of when you were a kid. Try and recall something you wanted to do or be back then, before the trials of teenage school, work, the profanity of adult life, drinking and drugs ever presented themselves as enticing. What did you want to be then? Picture that person, that old dream as 'you in the future'.

The key is to think of a 'future you' that you can be proud of and feel great as. When you have that image, spend five minutes thinking of that person and ways you can be like them. Ask the universe, or your god, yourself, or even just the ether to help you make decisions more aligned with that person. Ask the ether to please grant you this image and opportunities to be like that. Then ask for a better understanding of how to do that, and to be that.

STEP TWO

Throughout the day, when you come across a decision that makes you feel like you may be making a choice between right and wrong, stop. Are you in danger of feeling frustrated or shorthanded? Make the right choice. Ask the ether, yourself, god, or the universe, to give you strength and courage to make the choice. Ask for the frustration, anger, temptation, or jealousy to be lifted from you and for help to free you from the selfishness in making the wrong choice.

Maybe you're tempted in taking a nap instead of playing with your kid. Maybe it is having a drink that's enticing you to forget about going for a walk. Maybe watching television could keep you from looking for that job. Ask! Now do! Pretend your body is an engine that always has to be cold cranked. Do this everyday, one hour at a time, you just have to make it to the end of the day.

The key is not in believing in whoever or whatever it is your praying to. The key is in the action of asking for help. It reminds you that you have a decision, and allows you to make it. It also shifts the power from whatever object or substance it is in, away to something else that you are asking.

STEP THREE

Get on your knees right beside where you are about to lay your head for the night and picture the same thing you did in step one. This time silently say, "Thank you" to whatever might be listening, even if it may only be yourself. You want to be thankful for making it through a day. If you've made only choices that will lead you to a better understanding of who or what it is you envision for the future, be thankful for that. You want to say, "Thank you" directly to that imaginary person for being there as a possibility for you to strive toward. You want to thank whatever entity it is, if you have one, for providing you with the experiences necessary to achieve peace and happiness.

Thankfulness leaves no room for negativity and it is important to captures that energy at night before you lay down and let your body recover. You want to slowly form into an intricate and beautiful snowflake—night after night, day after day.

Jay Horne

A NOTE ON SUICIDE

The Only Thing I Like About Living

Jay Horne

Thoughts of suicide are real. I can't go as far as assuming that everyone has had them, because I am not everyone. The loss of hope can literally be a living hell and any advice I can give to those that feel hopeless, likely feel like hell is inescapable. What do you say to the man on death row to offer him consolation? What can you say to a mother who lost a child and blames herself for not plugging a hidden outlet in her home? Some things, experiences, that life has in its lottery bag, are hard to understand.

The only comfort I have ever found has been in a future where the same horrible experiences can be staved off from happening again. After the worst experience in my life, I was both terrified and jovial. The fear and memory associated with the pain of the event forced me to remember it forever. I swore the moment I knew that I would survive that I would never go through that again. But something else scared me. The thought of not having control over the possibility of re-living the experience. That is what truly scared me. "What if," I asked myself, "I die one day and am reborn into the exact same life, destined to live this all over again?" The thought terrified me.

I was thinking of something that may not come around for another one hundred years, and I was absolutely paralyzed with the thought of it. It took a few months for me to come to grips with the fear being a real possibility. Who knows what might become of us long after we die? Do we eventually get bored with heaven, or nothingness and CHOOSE to do it all again, either as something else or as the only other option, ourselves, again?

I knew for sure, that I didn't want that if it meant going through my worst fear again. So, I started affirming to myself that I would never willingly close a circle of my own existence. With that affirmation came a unique realization, for me, that I would never commit suicide. The only thing I had left standing between me and the worse experience in existence was time.

The more I thought about it, the more I decided that, no matter what my past had been, no matter how many wrongs I had done or had done to me, and no matter how many disappointments I had experienced, I still had my years left here to seek out an experience which might make it all worth it.

The Only Thing I Like About Living

Beyond that, I may even have the time after my death to find such an experience. To risk starting it all over now would be to live again through all of the disappointing, scary, and downright depressing years that had led me to the thoughts I had about suicide. Finally, I couldn't comprehend how it would help me any longer and I was freed.

I can never tell another human being, for sure, what they will go through during their lives or after their ends, but I am certain that the time we have allotted to us here should be fully explored. There may be an experience waiting for us in the last second of the last day of a life of a hundred years that makes us say to ourselves, "This life is the best thing that has ever happened to me, and I will never forget it."

I do know for sure that the opposite was possible for me, so such an experience must exist. Who knows, maybe memories so strong that you bring them past the grave are the true catalysts to the Spirit's growth.

A Persian philosopher named Julal as-Din Muhammad Rumi once said,

"I died as a mineral and became a plant. I died as a plant and rose to animal. I died as an animal and I was a man. Why should I fear? When was I less by dying?"

It is never shameful to reach out for help when thoughts of suicide arise. It is important to know that we are never truly alone. At the beginning of every AA meeting we make a declaration as a group.

I am responsible. Whenever, wherever someone reaches out for help, I want the hand of AA always to be there, and for that, I am responsible.

Even therapists themselves, doctors, and fire fighters all have resources for dependency, depression, and suicide. Most of those resources are staffed by people who have had similar suicidal thoughts in their history, and helping someone else with those problems helps them. It is sometimes the most powerful step in recovery to share your journey with another person. When newcomers fail to call the phone numbers which were freely given at AA, they fail to understand that they are robbing another addict of one of the most empowering and precious experiences offered to the recovering addict. The experience of sharing the things that keep them free of depression, addiction, and suicidal thoughts and actions. Sharing our experience is to express its truth and nothing is more human than truly expressing something we have only had a concept about.

    Reach out. There are tons of resources available to us today.

The Only Thing I Like About Living

RESOURCES FOR ADDICTION, SPIRITUALITY, AND SUICIDE

Alcoholics Anonymous Master Website
(Here you can find meetings and download all kinds of literature and information)
https://www.aa.org/

Substance Abuse and Mental Health Services Administration
(This is a great place to start your research if you are looking for an in-patient or out-patient mental health treatment center)
https://www.samhsa.gov/

Suicide Prevention Hotline
(Reach out here if you have thoughts of suicide or know someone who does)
1-800-273-8255

Get help with addiction at Project Know
https://www.projectknow.com/research/resources/
1-877-959-4415

To learn more about becoming like God check out this old book on Kabbalah
https://www.amazon.com/Becoming-Like-God-Kabbalah-Ultimate-ebook/dp/B07CNJLKYV

The Only Thing I Like About Living

Jay Horne

MY PERSONAL BELIEFS AND A NOTE ON ENLIGHTNEMENT

The Only Thing I Like About Living

Jay Horne

1

Readers often ask me about what I believe and in what I find my personal power to abstain. I think that everyone has to come into their own rock solid belief through a multitude of experiences. Only personal experiences can ever really prove a thing to you.

I use to read a lot of books on magic, Druidism, Celtic practices, and new age material when I was in my teens. I once read a story about how the bones of a dragon were kept in secret out on a little island in Wales. Because the island was supposedly nestled among a rocky stretch of treacherous land masses off the coast of Dragon's isle, few knew of its location and fewer were ever granted to see the bones. It was a fantastical story, but I liked it. I didn't necessarily believe it was true, but one day I was in the library and had been flipping through a huge atlas when I decided to do a little research. I couldn't turn up anything looking for Dragon's isle in modern depictions of Wales, but when I looked at historical information I found that the Isle of Wight used to go by that name. Flipping back to a modern map of Wales, I was excited to find there was an Isle of Wight, and directly off its coast stretched a length of rocky land masses referred to as The Needles.

That experience was over twenty five years ago and I will never forget that moment. It was the first time in my life that an idea had became more solid through my own genuine experience. This discovery made those writings real for me. As an adult I know now that the writer could have been well aware of the information and intentionally based the story on the simple fact (it is a technique I use in my fiction to this day) but I use the example to show the difference between believing something and knowing it.

I call my denomination, if you will, Gnostic.

I can only claim to have come upon a peculiar and on-going set of experiences that have led me to believe, with total conviction, what I am about to lay forth. Like most, I never had a problem with not knowing what the truth was about God or religion. I quite simply, did not care. However, it was hard not to be aware of all of the people in our lives that had some kind of true conviction to a belief or deity; they were everywhere.

The Only Thing I Like About Living

      Was it some experience that drove them to these convictions? Some guilt they were unable to shed? Some vision of grandeur which they had witnessed? Some miracle? Of course, there have been stages in my life when I wanted to believe. There have been sometimes that I wanted to believe so badly that I would have gladly played the fainting victim at the hands of the on-stage evangelist, just to see if 'faking it till ya make it' would work... Yet still, I just could not see a deity, know a deity, believe in a deity.
      I suppose the word Agnostic is a relatively new term, because I had not heard it then. It seems to me that Agnostics are the group of people that largely do not know that they are even included as part of the religious group, labeled as such. That makes it funny to think of. The term Agnostic quite literally means 'Those who do not know'.
      I came across the word Gnostic in a book by [Douglas Monroe](#), long before I ever read the word Agnostic. It means, of course, 'Those who know', and it was a word that encompassed a spiritual group of ancient Celtic origin. I think I first saw the word Agnostic as an option on my list of religious preferences while filling out paperwork at a blood blank; contrarily, Gnostic was not listed. "Whatever", I checked the square by the word 'none'. They took my blood either way, and the only thing nearing a spiritual revelation I had from the experience was being reminded that my blood type was 'B Positive'. That really should act as a constant affirmation for me, since I am mostly a negative and sarcastic thinking individual. Have I always been thus? I don't think entirely so. Between the ages of 27 and 35 my later personality gradually attached itself to my psyche.

2

Over the course of many years I experienced some big 'wow' moments that solidified my beliefs. The largest of which was my moment of enlightenment. The complete experience is recounted in numerous of my other books, but it was an experience, as such, that I truly know can never be forgotten. My hope is that even death can not strip the memory from me. The moment, which was smeared out over an area unimaginable in size, consisted of the worst and best experiences in existence. They are once in a lifetime because the chances of them occurring in the same way, and my soul surviving them, are impossibly improbable. I know not if everyone eventually experiences this kind of enlightenment but I think I understand what it is.

Enlightenment is in the letting go of every conception that you have of what is going on with the process you are undertaking. When enlightenment is realized, the totality of letting go envelops your whole experience and pure being takes over. What was known as life, or experience, becomes automated and the spirit is able to cleanly observe the process of existence as it moves and become aware of the meaning of it all. The opposite of this total enlightenment might be considered to be something akin to professional training in athletics or martial arts, for example. The focus of the feet hitting the ground with perfection, the awareness of moving opponents and targets, and the split second decisions to take actions can all mask the meaning behind existence.

During training, the observe is giving existence meaning. During enlightenment the observer is witnessing it. Beyond that, the spiritual master who is aware of the act of witnessing existence, can choose to give meaning to what is observed and manifest his thoughts into his experience. During enlightenment the person undergoing the process will find themselves in awe of the unlimited knowledge and understanding of how the universe works in conjunction with their own consciousness.

The dichotomy that is prevalent during this phase is one: the enlightened is aware of their power to choose any experience they would like – and two: the enlightened has no

The Only Thing I Like About Living

need for physical desires of the flesh for the mere act of wanting a certain experience conflicts with their position of pure choice.

Enlightenment is to marvel at the understanding that you are one with the universe. That you control your experience by controlling your thoughts about it. That you are ahead of judgement at every moment.

Why are the enlightened always envisioned as mystics meditating under a tree or monks, solitary on a mountain top? Because during the course of enlightenment there is no need to express your understanding of your world. The world is 'yours', in a sense. There would be no reason to tell someone that they should join you in enlightenment, because when you are in the midst of it, everyone and everything is part of your enlightenment.

I think that enlightenment is misunderstood because people expect someone to reach enlightenment like the Buddha and vanish into a blessed realm forever. While this is also possible, through one's choosing while experiencing the divine, it is less likely for someone who is bound to the ground for other spiritual or physical reasons. In my opinion, enlightenment is not something you reach and keep it forever—at least not until the end. I think that enlightenment is more of a temporary possession of infinite knowledge. It is why I am able to write about the experience after having it.

Positive living after the experience of enlightenment is a lot like how the body deals with a wounded hand. After a deep cut is inflicted on the skin of the palm, a sore and solid scab will appear over the injury. If the hand is utilized while the wound heals, the brittle scab will break at every crease that is flexed while making a fist. The breaks in the scab will run with fresh blood each time the fist is made, but over time, the flesh will heal with stronger, thicker, and more flexible skin. If the wound, instead, is left for weeks without being irritated and given time to heal, a scar may form and the flesh will always remain tender there.

After enlightenment the Gnostic is well aware that a rift in the soul has been scabbed and it is prevalent in his day to day life. After a brief enlightenment the flexing of the scab is necessary to lead to the long enlightenment. During the time of walking in the knowledge of enlightenment the Gnostic must practice his knowing by exercising positive thought and focusing on emptiness and non-preference. To have no preference is to have peace.

In closing, I would like to leave you with two tidbits of personal information.

A long time motto of mine: When it comes to the point I begin to slip into irritation, I remind myself:

Never favor.

and finally, an affirmation that I have never found to let me down:

I will be pleasantly surprised.

Good luck and God speed.

The Only Thing I Like About Living

Jay Horne

If you would like to know more about Jay Horne's spiritual journey, you can start with:
Life's a Joke!
His first novel while struggling with addiction and self-awareness.

Thank you for enjoying
THE ONLY THING I LIKE ABOUT LIVING

Written by: Jay Horne

For more information on the author visit his website at
http://www.jaymhorne.com

Questions or comments?
Your opinion is important to us!
Contact the publisher at:
http://www.bookflurry.com

Please be sure to leave a review at:
Amazon.com

The Only Thing I Like About Living

Referenced Hyperlinks:

https://castaneda.com/
https://www.amazon.com/Rhode-Island-Novelty-JBWWJD4-Bracelets/dp/B00KBBFXB4
https://www.amazon.com/Kundalini-Awakening-Gentle-Activation-Spiritual/dp/0553353306
https://www.amazon.com/As-Waffle-Burns-Jay-Horne/dp/1460955056
https://www.amazon.com/Conversations-God-Uncommon-Dialogue-Book/dp/0399142789
http://www.unitedearth.com.au/watercrystals.html
https://www.amazon.com/Alcoholics-AAWS/dp/1893007162
http://www.proust-ink.com/biography/
https://www.aa.org/assets/en_US/smf-121_en.pdf
http://singaporeaa.org/PDFs/The_AA_Promises.pdf
http://www.rumi.net/
https://www.amazon.com/21-Lessons-Merlyn-Study-Druid-ebook/dp/B004FV67WA

The Only Thing I Like About Living

Made in the USA
Las Vegas, NV
06 April 2025